WHAT DOES THE US PRESIDENT DO?

GOVERNMENT LESSONS FOR KIDS
Children's Government Books

Speedy Publishing LLC

40 E. Main St. #1156

Newark, DE 19711

www.speedypublishing.com

Copyright 2017

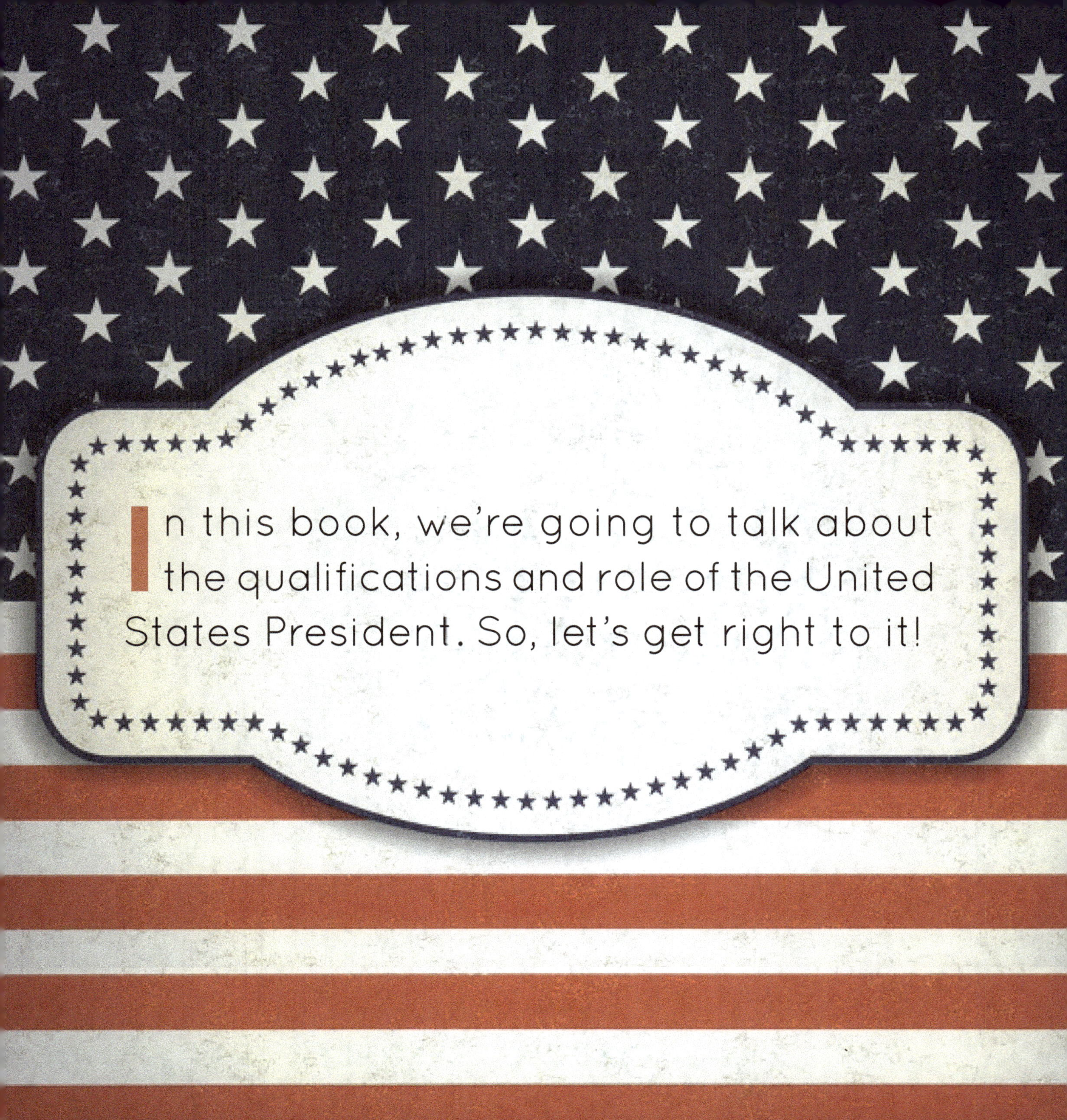

In this book, we're going to talk about the qualifications and role of the United States President. So, let's get right to it!

Although there are lots of people involved in the government of the United States, there's only one President. The job of United States President is very demanding.

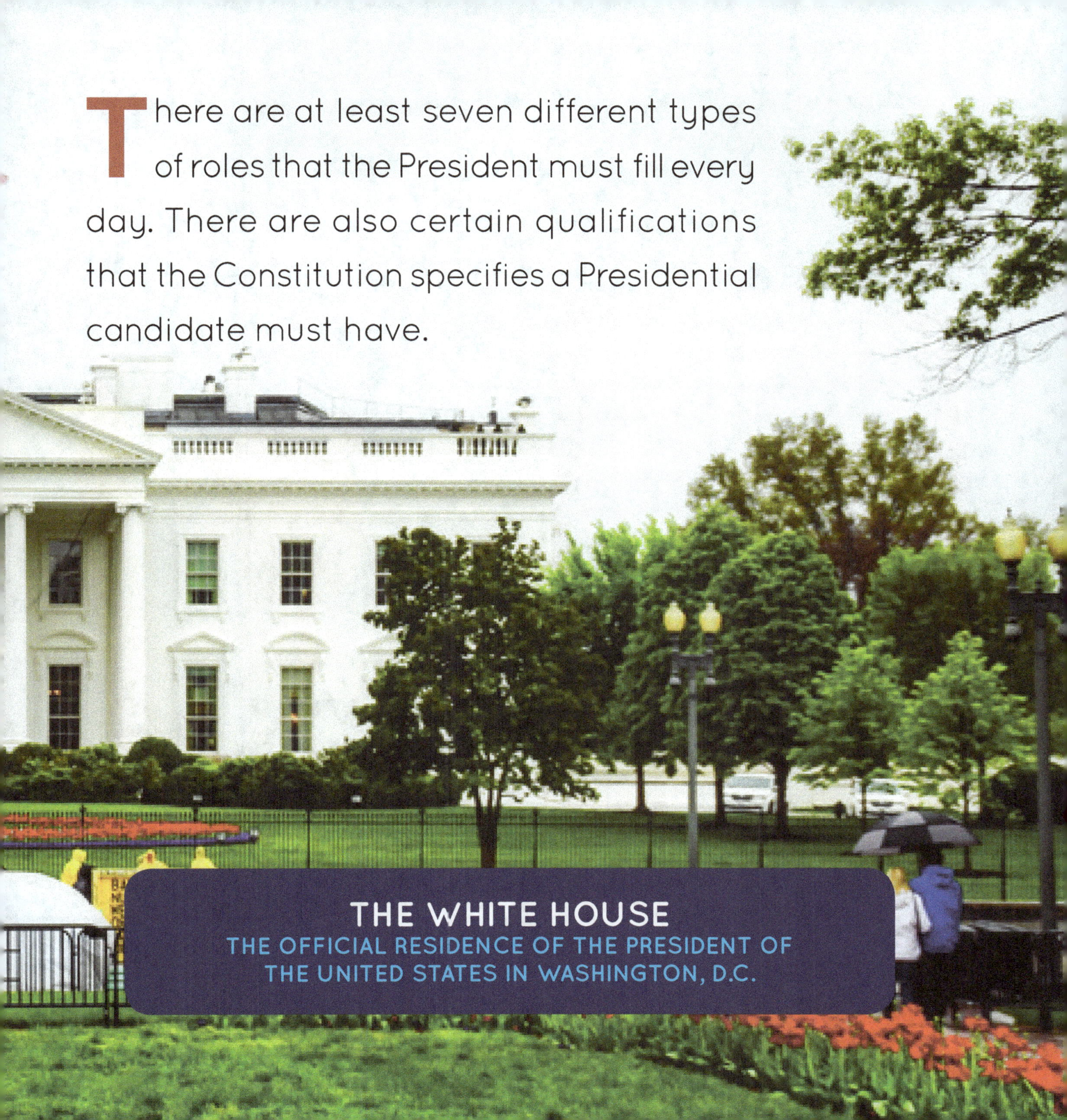

There are at least seven different types of roles that the President must fill every day. There are also certain qualifications that the Constitution specifies a Presidential candidate must have.

WHAT QUALIFICATIONS DOES A PRESIDENT NEED TO HAVE?

The United States Constitution explains the exact requirements that an individual must have in order to become a presidential candidate. There are three basic requirements:

- ☑ The candidate must be at least 35 years of age.
- ☑ The candidate must have been born in the United States.
- ☑ The candidate must have been a United States resident for a minimum of 14 years.

Most Presidents have been 50 years old or older when they became elected. President John F. Kennedy was the youngest President ever elected.

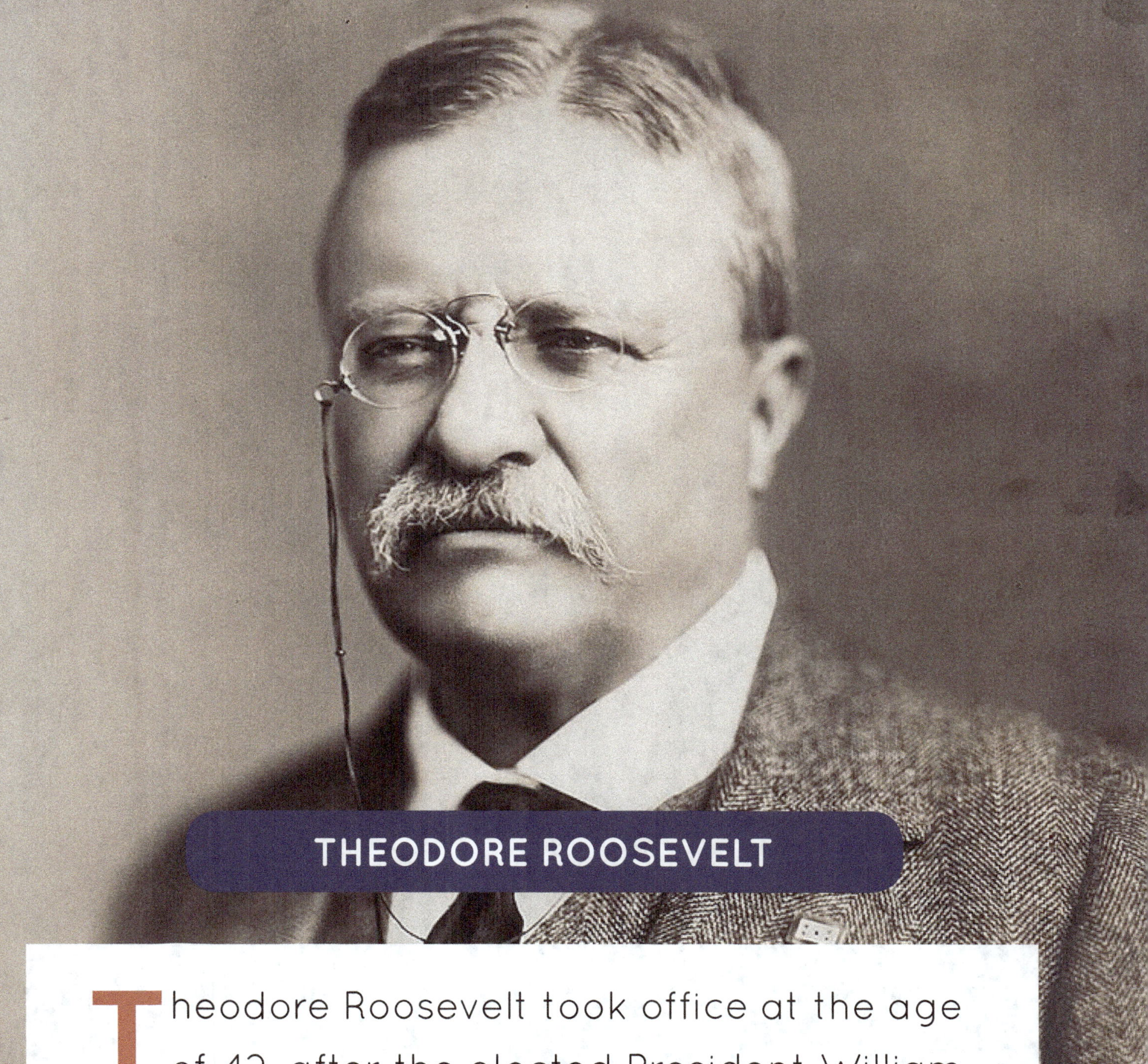

Theodore Roosevelt took office at the age of 42, after the elected President William McKinley was assassinated.

PRESIDENT DONALD TRUMP

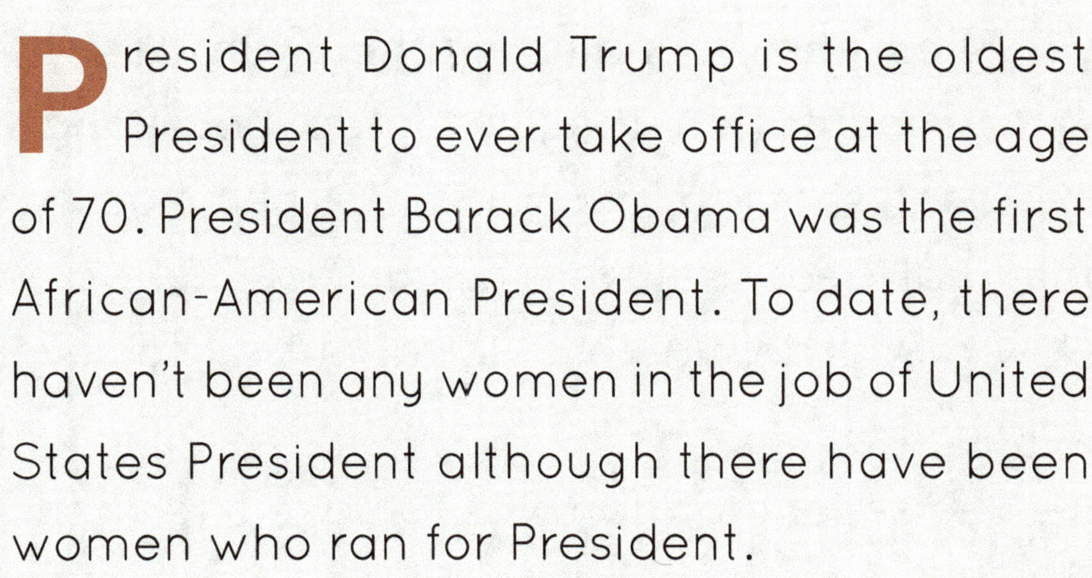

President Donald Trump is the oldest President to ever take office at the age of 70. President Barack Obama was the first African-American President. To date, there haven't been any women in the job of United States President although there have been women who ran for President.

HOW LONG CAN A PRESIDENT SERVE IN OFFICE?

When the Founding Fathers drafted the Constitution they debated how long a President should stay in office. They had two potential ideas that were discussed. One was to allow a Presidential term for about six to seven years.

The second option was to have a term that lasted four years, with the possibility of the President being elected again. They decided on the second option. At that time, they didn't set any limit on the number of times a President could be re-elected.

EISENHOWER CHIEF OF STAFF
PORTRAIT

FRANKLIN DELANO ROOSEVELT

President Franklin Delano Roosevelt served four terms in succession, which was a total of 16 years as President during the 1940s. However, many people felt that a President shouldn't hold the office for that long. To change the Constitution, Congress drafted the 22nd Amendment, which was approved by the states.

It limits the number of terms to two. That means a President can only serve a total of eight years as President. If something happens to the President and the Vice President takes over, then that individual can serve for the remainder of the Presidency and then be elected to two more terms after that.

The 22nd Amendment is still controversial today. President Truman, President Eisenhower, and President Reagan all wanted it to be changed. They thought that the American people should have the ultimate say on how long a person should be President.

DWIGHT D. EISENHOWER

HARRY S. TRUMAN
They also said that the President's authority is weakened at the end of the second term because the people know that the President's time in office will soon be over.

Those citizens who are in favor for the Amendment believe that it prevents any one individual from gaining too much power.

WHAT DOES THE PRESIDENT EARN?

According to the United States Code, Title 3, the United States President receives a yearly salary of $400,000. The President also receives an annual expense account of $50,000. There's a $100,000 travel account that's not taxable and a $19,000 allowance for entertainment.

HERBERT HOOVER

This may seem like a tremendous amount of money for a government official who is elected to serve the people, but it is far less than many heads of corporations earn. Some Presidents, such as President John F. Kennedy and President Herbert Hoover, donated their salaries to charity.

There are also other benefits that the President receives. The President and his or her family get free housing in the White House and free transportation by land in the

Presidential limousine, by sea in Marine One, and by air, in Air Force One. After they serve in office, Presidents receive an annual pension of $200,000 annually.

AERIAL VIEW OF U.S. AIR FORCE ONE BOEING 747

PRESIDENT RICHARD NIXON

WHAT DOES THE PRESIDENT'S JOB ENTAIL?

The President's job is very difficult and challenging. Although the Constitution partially outlines the responsibilities of the Presidency, technology and the demands of modern society have placed more expectations on the role of President than ever before. There are seven major roles that Presidents fulfill in their position.

CHIEF OF STATE

The American people expect that their President will set an inspiring example not only for the United States, but also for all countries around the globe. In some nations, the Chief of State role is filled by a monarch who wears regal robes and a crown on special occasions. In many countries, such as England and Japan, the Chief of State fulfills this role without ruling over the government.

The United States President doesn't wear a crown or special clothes, but does celebrate national holidays and, more importantly, is a symbol of the United States.

It's a great honor for anyone around the world to shake the hand of the President of the United States.

In his or her role as Chief of State, the United States President might award a medal to an outstanding college student, shake the hands of the United States astronauts before they journey into space, or give a rousing, patriotic speech during a Fourth of July celebration.

FAMILY ON FOURTH OF JULY

We the People
insure domestic Tranquility, provide for the common defence,
and our Posterity, do ordain and establish this Constitution
Section. 1. All legislative Powers herein granted shall be

CHIEF EXECUTIVE

In order to keep a system of checks and balances within the United States government, there are three branches.

- ⮐ The Executive Branch, which consists of the President and some 5 million government workers.
- ⮐ The Legislative Branch, which consists of the Senate as well as the House of Representatives.
- ⮐ The Judicial Branch, which consists of the Supreme Court as well as other lower courts.

As the head of one of the three branches of the government, the executive branch, the President is responsible for the day-to-day running of the federal government. He or she enforces the laws that have been passed by Congress. In order to do this effectively, the President needs other people in important government positions.

LEGISLATIVE

EXECUTIVE

JUDICIAL

He or she appoints individuals to key positions and nominates cabinet members. The individuals appointed to the President's cabinet are the heads of the main executive departments of the government. They also help advise the President on important policy matters.

In this role, the President also appoints the leaders of important agencies, as well as federal judges and a host of about 2,000 other positions. The Senate needs to approve the President's choices for these positions, but the President also has the power to fire an individual who is not fulfilling his or her job to a successful level. In his or her role as Chief Executive, the President might appoint the leader of the Central Intelligence Agency, summon a meeting with the cabinet to get advice on a government issue, or study reports about problems within the Federal Bureau of Investigation.

ABRAHAM LINCOLN CARICATURE

PRESIDENT BARACK OBAMA SIGNS THE
UNITED STATES-ISRAEL ENHANCED
SECURITY COOPERATION ACT

CHIEF DIPLOMAT

The President makes the decisions regarding the policies communicated to the governments of foreign nations through American diplomats as well as ambassadors. He or she also creates the foreign policies of the United States government with the help of cabinet members and other advisors.

In his or her role as Chief Diplomat, the President might entertain diplomats from Japan with a dinner at the White House, travel to Britain to meet with members of the royal family, or write an important letter to the government leaders in Russia.

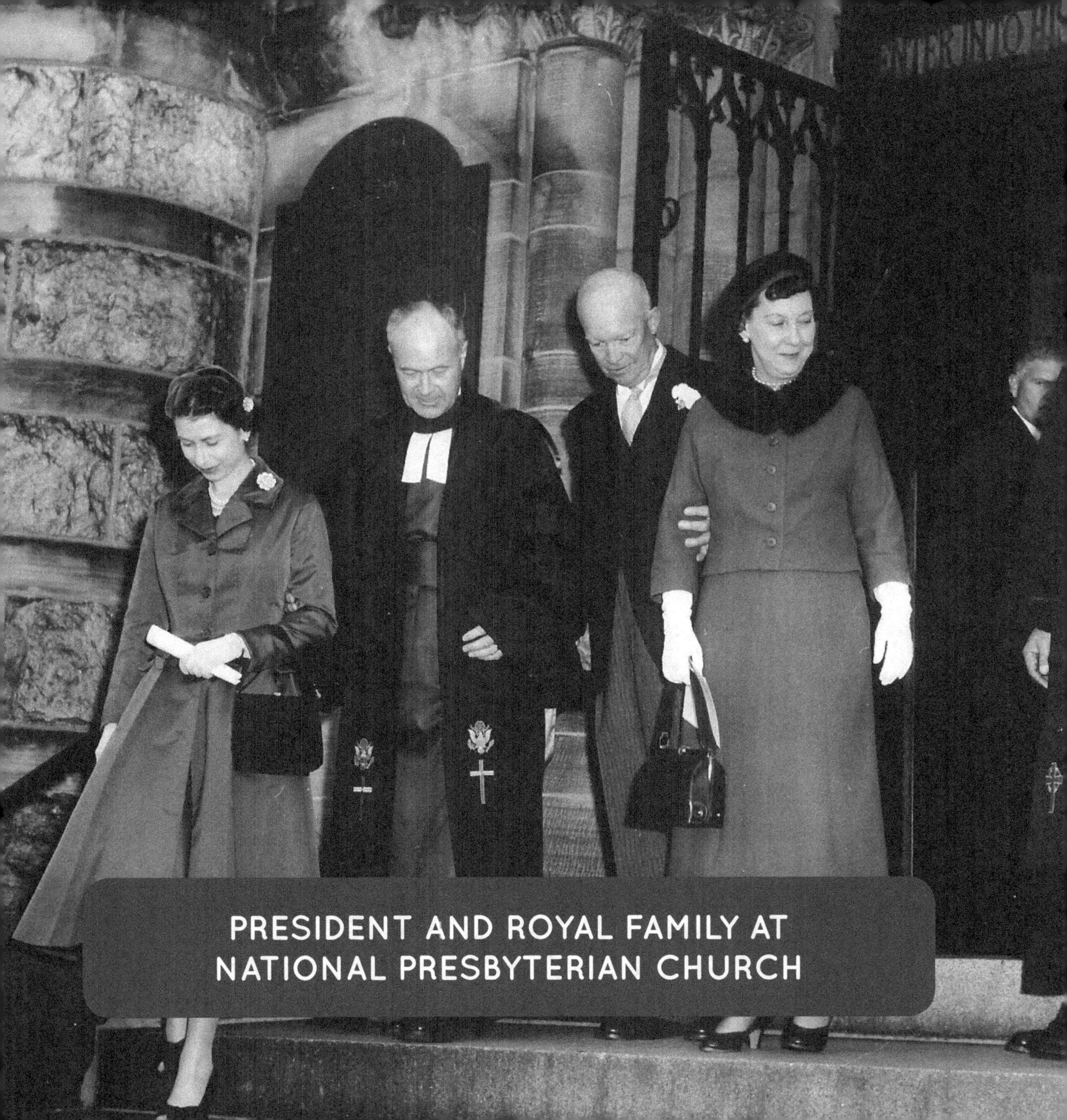

PRESIDENT AND ROYAL FAMILY AT
NATIONAL PRESBYTERIAN CHURCH

PRESIDENT OBAMA

COMMANDER-IN-CHIEF

The President is the leader of all the United States Armed Forces on land, on sea, and in the air. The President makes decisions about where United States troops will be stationed as well as where ships or planes are sent, and how destructive weapons will be deployed.

All heads of the military including army generals and navy admirals get their military orders from the President. In his or her role as Commander-in-Chief, the President might conduct an inspection of a Navy yard, make a decision about whether a bomb should be dropped on an enemy's city, or deploy troops to halt a riot at the request of a state's governor.

PRESIDENT BUSH WITH
THE US NAVY

PRESIDENT GEORGE W. BUSH ADDRESSES
JOINT SESSION OF CONGRESS

LEGISLATIVE LEADER

Even though Congress proposes and makes the laws of the country, the President still has an influence on which bills are signed into law and which are not. The President can encourage Congress to draft and pass certain laws. The President also has the power to veto any bills that he or she doesn't want to pass. In his or her role as Legislative Leader, the President might sign a bill into law, veto a bill that he or she didn't want to pass, or make a speech in front of Congress.

CHIEF OF PARTY

The President helps members of his or her party, either Democrat or Republican, get elected to positions. The President campaigns for those leaders who have supported the party's policies. At the end of a President's first term, he or she may campaign to be re-elected for a second term. In this role, the President might choose members of his or her party to serve as Cabinet members or travel to New York to speak in support of a party's choice for United States Senate.

BARACK OBAMA
PRESIDENTIAL CAMPAIGN

PROSPERITY
AT HOME, PRESTIGE ABROAD.
COMMERCE.
CIVILIZATION

GUARDIAN OF THE ECONOMY

The economy of the United States is very important, and the citizens of the United States expect the President to be watchful about issues that could have a detrimental effect on the economy.

He or she doesn't control the economy but must do everything possible to see that it's running smoothly.

In this role, the President might discuss ways to reduce the level of unemployment or meet with important business owners to discuss their pressing problems.

THE U.S. PRESIDENT HAS MANY ROLES

The United States President is the head of one of three branches of the government. There are seven different roles that the President must fulfill on a daily basis. Being President is a very demanding position.

Awesome! Now that you've learned about what the United States President does, you may want to read about the first President of the United States in the Baby Professor book George Washington: The Father of His Country – History You Should Know.

Visit

BABY PROFESSOR
EDUCATION KIDS

www.BabyProfessorBooks.com

to download Free Baby Professor eBooks
and view our catalog of new and exciting
Children's Books